Illustrations: *Raquel Sonera*
Formatt: *Alba D. Reboyras*
Color enhancing: *Jafet Reboyras*

To request additional copies or obtain this book in digital version, write to *soneraraquel97@gmail.com*

DEDICATION

FIRST AND FOREMOST, THIS BOOK IS DEDICATED TO ALL MY LOVING ANIMAL FRIENDS THAT HAPPILY RESIDE AT THE SANCTUARY.
SECONDLY, THIS BOOK IS DEDICATED TO DR. SANKAR SASTRI THE COW-PASSIONATE FOUNDER OF LAKSHMI COW AND ANIMAL SANCTUARY.
I LOVE MOO SANKAR FOR YOUR DEDICATION TO SERVING AND PROTECTING THE COWS AND OTHER ANIMALS. YOUR MISSION TO RESCUE AND PROVIDE ANIMALS WITH A LOVING HOME ON 92 ACRES OF LAND FOR THE REST OF THEIR LIVES MAKES YOU A RARE AND BEAUTIFUL SOUL.
LASTLY, THIS BOOK IS DEDICATED TO ALL THE KIND, HARDWORKING, SERVICE ORIENTED SANCTUARY VOLUNTEERS (PAST, PRESENT, AND FUTURE). THANK YOU EDYE HUANG FOR BEING A DEVOTED VOLUNTEER FOR TEN OF THOSE YEARS.

ACKNOWLEDGEMENT

OCEANS OF THANKS TO ALBA REBOYRAS FOR FORMATTING, AND SELF-PUBLISHING THIS BOOK. YOU ARE A TRUE BLESSING, AND ANSWER TO MY PRAYERS!
MY DEEPEST GRATITUDE TO JAFET REBOYRAS FOR DIGITALLY COLOR ENHANCING ALL OF MY ARTWORK. GOD BLESS YOU!

HELLO WELCOME! NAMASTE! THE THREE OF US LIVE HAPPILY HERE AT LAKSHMI COW AND ANIMAL SANCTUARY. MY NAME IS BRAHMA STANDING TO THE LEFT. BRAHMA IS THE HINDU GOD MEANING THE CREATOR OF THE UNIVERSE.

MY NAME IS VISHNU STANDING IN THE MIDDLE. VISHNU IS THE HINDU GOD THAT IS THE PRESERVER OF CREATION.

MY NAME IS SHIVA STANDING TO THE RIGHT. SHIVA IS THE HINDU GOD MEANING THE DESTROYER OF THE UNIVERSE IN ORDER TO RECREATE IT.

ALL THE ANIMALS AT LAKSHMI COW AND ANIMAL SANCTUARY ARE NAMED AFTER HINDU GODS AND GODDESSES. WHENEVER HUMAN BEINGS ARE VISITING AND CALLING US BY OUR SPIRITUAL NAME THE DIVINE IS ALWAYS ACKNOWLEDGED.

HI MY NAME IS CRYSTAL DURGA. I AM A TEXAS LONGHORN. I LOVE IT AT THE ANIMAL SANCTUARY BECAUSE I FEEL SAFE. I AM VERY LOVED AND CARED FOR HERE INSTEAD OF EATEN. I DON'T BECOME SOMEBODY'S MEAL.
I AM SURE YOU KNOW HOW I FEEL. HOW WOULD YOU LIKE BECOMING DINNER ON SOMEONE'S PLATE?

HI MY NAME IS LAVA. I COMMUNICATE WITH THE SANCTUARY FOUNDER SANKAR. WE SPEAK THE SAME LANGUAGE AND HE UNDERSTANDS MY NEED FOR FREEDOM. SANKAR DOES NOT MIND IF I COME AND GO. HE DOES OCCASIONALLY ASK ME TO JOIN IN AT COMMUNITY EVENTS.

I MAKE THE DECISION TO SPEND TIME WITH THE KIND PEOPLE THAT VISIT. THEY LOVE ANIMALS, INCLUDING ME A TURKEY! I DON'T BECOME THEIR THANKSGIVING MEAL AND I AM EXTREMELY GRATEFUL FOR THAT!

HI MY NAME IS LITTLE GIRL GOVINDA. DON'T LET THE NAME FOOL YOU. I AM ACTUALLY ABOUT 20 YEARS OLD. I MOVE A LITTLE SLOWER NOW SO THE COW-PASSIONATE VOLUNTEERS SPECIAL DELIVER WATER, GRAINS, AND HAY TO ME OVER IN THE PASTURE.

I LOVE IT THE MOST WHEN THEY BRING ME SPECIAL TREATS LIKE BANAN-AS, APPLES, AND SOMETIMES EVEN WATERMELON! THIS MAKES ME FEEL LIKE A V.I.C. VERY IMPORTANT COW!

HI MY NAME IS GITA. I HAVE LIVED AT THE SANCTUARY FOR TEN OR MORE YEARS. SOMETIMES I LIKE TO RELAX AT THE WINDOWSILL AND BASK IN THE MEOW-VELOUS SUNLIGHT.

SOME DAYS I LIKE EXPLORING THE MANY DIFFERENT GREEN PASTURES, AND SAYING HELLO TO ALL MY COW FRIENDS. THEY ARE MOO-VELOUS!

HI MY NAME IS HANUMAN. I HAVE LIVED AT THE SANCTUARY FOR TEN OR MORE YEARS LIKE MY FRIEND GITA. I LOVE THE OUTDOORS! I LOVE EXPLORING THE FRAGRANT PASTURES, BARNS, AND INSIDE THE OLD FARMHOUSE. I AM FRIENDLY TO BOTH THE GUESTS AND VOLUN-TEERS. I ROLL AROUND IN THE GRASS AT THEIR FEET AND PAY MY HUMBLE OBEISANCES TO THEM.

THE SPRING AND SUMMER MONTHS MY FOOD IS DELIVERED TO THE BARN. I COME RUNNING FOR BREAKFAST AND DINNER. THE FALL AND WINTER MONTHS THE WEATHER IS MUCH COLDER AND I GET TO ROOM INSIDE THE HOUSE. I SLEEP IN A WARM, COZY BED WITH ONE OF THE VOLUNTEERS. SOMETIMES WE PLAY HIDE AND GO SEEK TOGETHER. I LOVE TO PLAY! MANY TIMES VOLUNTEERS WILL FIND A STRING AND SWIRL IT AROUND. I QUICKLY PAW AND POUNCE ON IT.

HI I AM SHIVA DANNY! I AM A JERSEY COW. I HAVE THE SACRED OM SYMBOL ON THE SIDE OF MY FACE. I LOVE MY LIFE HERE AT LAKSHMI COW AND ANIMAL SANCTUARY. PEOPLE COME AND PET ME, BRUSH ME, AND GIVE ME HUGS.

I GIVE THEM COW KISSES AND COW CUDDLES IN RETURN. THEY LIKE TAKING "SELFIES" WITH ME. I LOVE ALL THE ATTENTION I RECEIVE WHEN I GET MY PICTURE TAKEN. I AM VERY PHOTO-MOO- GENIC! FRE- QUENTLY, PEOPLE BRING ME APPLES WHICH I DEVOUR! "AN APPLE A DAY KEEPS THE VETERINARIAN AWAY!"

HI MY NAME IS GANESH! I WAS FOUND IN THE KITCHEN BY A VOLUNTEER. THANK GOD SHE WAS NOT AFRAID OF ME. THE LANDOWNER SANKAR TOLD THE VOLUNTEER IT WAS FREEZING COLD OUTSIDE AND TO MAKE ME AN INDOOR HOME. THEY PLACED ME INSIDE A BUCKET WITH A LITTLE HAY, LEAVES, GRASS AND TWIGS.

I WAS FED GRAINS AND WATER. THEY CHECKED IN ON ME OFTEN, TALKED TO ME, AND PET ME. THEY TOOK GOOD CARE OF ME UNTIL THE WEATHER WARMED UP AND I COULD LIVE OUTSIDE AGAIN.

HI THERE! MY NAME IS DURGA. I AM A BARN CAT. I GUESS YOU COULD SAY I AM THE GODDESS OF THE BARN. I LOVE BEING AROUND THE BALES OF HAY.
THEY SMELL LIKE GRASS AND LAVENDER. I ALSO LIKE HANGING OUT WITH ALL MY COW FRIENDS THAT SPEND SO MUCH TIME INSIDE THE BARN. MANY VISITORS COME INSIDE THE BARN AND SCRATCH BEHIND MY EARS, AND PET ME ALL OVER. I PURR LOUDLY. I PLACE MY PAW ONTO THEIR CHEST. I WANT THEM TO KNOW THAT I LOVE THEM, AND I WANT THEM TO CONTINUE PETTING ME!

HI I AM VISHNU. HELLO MY NAME IS SHIVA. I AM A ROOSTER, AND I RULE THE ROOST BY WAKING UP THE VOLUNTEERS EARLY IN THE MORNING COCK-A-DOODLE-DOING!

I HELP THE VOLUNTEERS RISE AND SHINE EARLY SO THEY CAN START THEIR MORNING "SEVA" (SERVICE).

I AM BRAHMA OVER HERE. THIS IS OUR BRIGHT, SPACIOUS, LOVELY HOME. INSIDE THE COOP WE EAT TOGETHER, TALK, SLEEP, AND COME AND GO AS WE PLEASE.

HELLO AGAIN... IT'S ME CRYSTAL DURGA! I WAS JUST THINKING ABOUT MY MOM SARASVATI TODAY. SHE DIED A COUPLE OF YEARS AGO. I MISS HER A LOT.
I WILL ALWAYS HAVE SPECIAL MEMORIES I SHARED WITH HER AT THE SANCTUARY. I AM SO RELIEVED WE WERE NOT SEPARATED FROM EACH OTHER LIKE MANY HOLSTEIN COWS ARE THAT LIVE ON DAIRY FARMS. I WOULD HAVE FELT VERY SAD AND DEPRESSED. MY MOM WAS MY BEST FRIEND! SHE NURSED ME, TOLD ME MOO-TIME STORIES, GROOMED ME, AND KISSED ME EVERY NIGHT AT BEDTIME BEFORE I WENT TO SLEEP.

HI MY NAME IS BALARAM. I AM A JERSEY COW. I JUST WANT TO GIVE A QUICK SHOUT OUT TO ALL THE VOLUNTEERS AND THANK THEM FOR THEIR HELP HERE AT LAKSHMI COW AND ANIMAL SANCTUARY. THE VOLUNTEERS FEED US WATER, GRAINS, AND HAY TWICE DAILY.

THEY SHOVEL OUR COW DUNG AND CLEAN OUR BARNS. THEY PICK UP HEAVY ROCKS, AND ROCKS OF ALL SIZES SO WE WON'T STEP ON THEM. THEY BRUSH, PET, AND MASSAGE US DAILY. THEY HAVE MANY "TO MOO" PROJECTS ON THE FARM TO MAKE SURE WE ARE ALL WELL NURTURED AND CARED FOR WHILE WE LIVE OUT OUR LIVES HERE. THEY REMOVE STRING THAT IS ATTACHED TO THE HAY BALES SO WE WON'T EAT THEM AND GET SICK. THEY EVEN USE OUR COW DUNG TO MAKE PATTIES. THE DUNG IS SHAPED INTO PATTIES, SUN DRIED, PACK-AGED AND THEN SHIPPED TO PEOPLE TO USE IN THEIR HOMES FOR SACRED CEREMONIES SUCH AS HOMA, PUJA, AND AGNI HOTRA.

THE OTHER DAY I CHASED AFTER A VOLUNTEER THAT WAS DANGLING SOME CARROTS I WANTED TO EAT. I JUMPED OVER A TROUGH BARRI-CADE. THE BARRICADE WAS PLACED THERE SO MY FELLOW COW BUD-DIES WOULD NOT STEP INTO WET LIQUID CONCRETE. IT TURNED OUT THAT I LANDED RIGHT IN IT! SANKAR RINSED OFF MY LEGS RIGHT AWAY SO THAT THE WET CONCRETE WOULD NOT EAT AWAY AT MY SKIN. SANKAR IS UDDERLY CARING! I AM THANKFUL HE IS VERY CONCERNED FOR OUR SAFETY.

HI MY NAME IS SITA. I AM A HOLSTEIN COW. I AM IDENTIFIED BY THE HEART ON MY FOREHEAD. I AM A LITTLE SHY AND SPEND MORE TIME BY MYSELF. THE REST OF THE HERD IS VERY SOCIAL. I LOVE RELAXING IN THE GRASSY FIELDS.

IT IS HEAVENLY SMELLING THE SWEET FRAGRANCES OF NATURE, AND LISTENING TO THE BIRDS SING. I ENJOY BASKING IN THE WARM SUN, AND STARING UP AT THE EXPANSIVENESS OF THE BLUE SKY.

HI MY NAME IS RAMA. I AM A BRAHMA BULL. MOST PEOPLE RECOGNIZE ME BY THE LARGE HUMP ON MY BACK. I AM AN INDIAN BREED BULL. I HAVE MORE ACTIVE SWEAT GLANDS AND SECRETE AN OILY SECRETION THAT HELPS ME REPEL INSECTS.

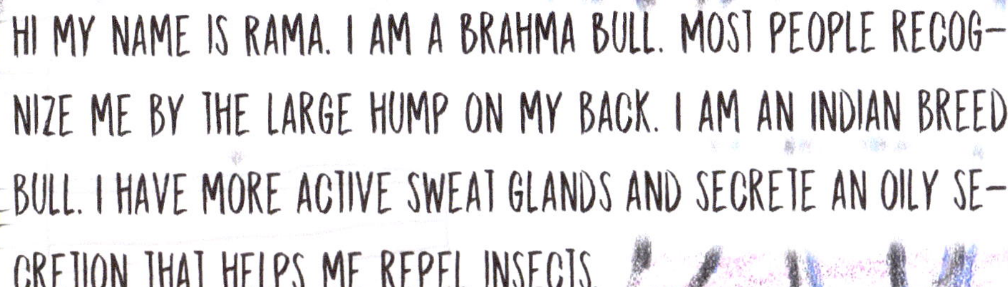

I AM A VERY FAST RUNNER. JUST THE OTHER DAY ABOUT THREE VOLUNTEERS WERE CHASING ME SO I COULD HAVE MY HOOVES TRIMMED. BOY DID I SURE GIVE THEM A RUN FOR THEIR MONEY. NONE OF THEM COULD CATCH ME. EVENTUALLY, I GAVE IN BECAUSE MY HOOVES WERE TOO LONG! I THOUGHT THEY REALLY COULD USE A TRIM. OVERGROWN HOOVES CAN BECOME VERY PAINFUL, AND I DON'T WANT A FOOT INJURY OR TO START LIMPING.

HI I AM MINA! MINA IS SHORT FOR MANAKSHI. I AM TAKING A BRIEF CAT NAP BEFORE I GO OUTDOORS AND EXPLORE! I LOVE LOTS OF FRESH AIR AND OUTDOOR ADVENTURES.

ESPECIALLY HERE AT THE SANCTUARY! THERE ARE SO MANY TREES TO CLIMB, HAY STACKS TO JUMP ON, COW DUNG TO SNIFF, AND 92 ACRES OF LAND.

I LOVE MOO

HI BLESSINGS! MY NAME IS YOGESHRI. I AM AN ADULT NOW, BUT WHEN I FIRST ARRIVED AT THE SANCTUARY AS A YOUNG CALF TWO VOLUNTEERS EMILY AND RACHEL WOULD MIX TOGETHER A MILK FORMULA FOR ME TO DRINK SO I WOULD RECEIVE ALL THE PROPER NUTRIENTS I NEEDED TO GROW.

THEY DID THIS FOR ME AND MY BEST FRIEND NANDINI. THE MILK FORMULA WAS PLACED IN A BUCKET WITH AN UDDER ATTACHED TO IT. NANDINI AND I WOULD COME RUNNING, AND NUDGE THE BUCKET OFTEN SPILLING SOME OF THE MILK ONTO THE VOLUNTEERS.

NANDINI AND I WERE SEPARATED FROM OUR MOTHERS AT BIRTH, AND THAT IS WHY WE WERE GIVEN THE MILK FORMULA AT THE SANCTUARY. WE TURNED OUT TO BE HEALTHY ADULTS, BUT I SURE DO WISH I COULD HAVE KNOWN MY MOTHER AND NURSED FROM HER NATURALLY. I FEEL HER WITH ME IN SPIRIT WATCHING OVER ME.

I THINK HER SPIRIT HELPED BRING ME TO LAKSHMI COW AND ANIMAL SANCTUARY. HERE I AM SAFE AND PROTECTED FOR THE REST OF MY LIFE.

HI BLESSINGS MY NAME IS LAKSHMI! I AM A JERSEY COW. MY SON NANDA AND I LIVE AT THE SANCTUARY. I LOVE HIM VERY MUCH. HE AND I ARE VERY CLOSE.

I AM VERY HAPPY HE AND I CAN LIVE TOGETHER HERE. RIGHT NOW I AM STAYING IN THE COZY EXTENSION PART OF THE HOUSE. I INJURED MY HIP AND IT IS DIFFICULT FOR ME TO WALK RIGHT NOW. THE LOVING VOLUNTEERS BRING MY MEALS TO ME SO THAT I DON'T HAVE TO WALK TO THE BARN AT MEAL TIMES.

YOU MAY THINK LAKSHMI COW AND ANIMAL SANCTUARY WAS NAMED AFTER ME, BUT IT WAS NOT. IT WAS NAMED AFTER A COW IN INDIA NAMED LAKSHMI. SHE HAD NINE CALVES OF HER OWN. LAKSHMI WAS GREATLY DEVOTED TO BHAGAVAN SRI RAMANA MAHARSHI ONE OF THE GREATEST SAGES AND TEACHERS OF INDIA.

DAILY LAKSHMI WOULD WALK MILES TO VISIT HIM AT HIS ASHRAM AND THEN GO BACK HOME. SHE WAS VERY DEVOTED TO BHAGAVAN, AND LOVED SITTING NEXT TO HIM. THEY COULD COMMUNICATE TELEPATHI-CALLY WITH ONE ANOTHER, AND THEIR RELATIONSHIP HAD A VERY LOVING ASSOCIATION.

HELLO NAMASTE! MY NAME IS VEDANTA. PEOPLE USUALLY RECOGNIZE ME BY THE QUESTION MARK IN THE CENTER OF MY FACE. THE FOLLOWING IS A QUOTE BY BHAGAVAN RAMANA MAHARSHI:

"BY INCESSANTLY PURSUING WITHIN YOURSELF THE INQUIRY "WHO AM I?" YOU WILL KNOW YOUR TRUE SELF AND THEREBY ATTAIN SALVATION."

WHEN PEOPLE SEE ME AND THE QUESTION MARK ON MY FACE IT IS A REMINDER FOR SELF-INQUIRY, AND TO ASK THE QUESTION "WHO AM I?"

BHAGAVAN RAMANA MAHARSHI TEACHES THE FOLLOWING:

"WE ARE NOT THESE BODIES. WE ARE PURE AWARENESS, PURE CONSCIOUSNESS. I AM AWARENESS THAT KNOWS I AM HAVING THESE EXPERIENCES."

HI I AM NANDINI! YOU MET MY BEST FRIEND YOGESHRI EARLIER. SHE MENTIONED THAT WE WERE GIVEN MILK FORMULA AS CALVES. IT WAS PUT IN A BUCKET WITH AN UDDER ATTACHED TO IT. ALTERNATIVELY, THE FORMULA CAN BE PUT INTO BIG BABY BOTTLES AND WE CAN BE BOTTLED FED. THE BOTTLES PREVENT THE MILK FROM SPILLING.
ALTHOUGH I WAS SEPARATED FROM MY MOTHER AS A BABY, AS AN ADULT I HAVE BECOME A MOTHER TO MY OWN CALF THAT I AM ABLE TO NURSE. HER NAME IS SORABHI. SHE IS MY LIFE BLESSING FROM THE DIVINE.

HI MY NAME IS NAMAS-KAR. I AM A TYPICAL ROOSTER THAT LIKES TO WAKE UP EARLY.
I AM NAMASTE. MOST PEOPLE DISCOVER THAT I AM A HEN WHEN I LAY EGGS FROM TIME TO TIME. THE OTHER WAY YOU CAN TELL IS THAT THE COMB IS LARGER ON A ROOSTER`S HEAD. THE WATTLES (THE FLESHY SKIN THAT HANGS UNDERNEATH THE NECK) IS LARGER ON ROOSTERS TOO.

HI MY NAME IS MINA! I LOVE GOING OVER TO THE BALES OF HAY THAT HAVE A TARP DRAPED OVER THEM. THE HAYSTACKS ARE MY LOOKOUT POST. AFTER I LEAVE MY POST I ROLL AROUND IN THE GRASSY FIELDS, CHASE BUGS, AND DIG AROUND IN THE DIRT.

RAMA, THE BRAHMA BULL AND I LIKE TO CHASE AFTER EACH OTHER TOO. HE'S MY GOOD BUDDY. WE OFTEN GREET EACH OTHER WITH A FRIENDLY KISS. I RUN FAST, AND MAKE HIM CHASE AFTER ME IF HE WANTS A SECOND KISS.

HI I AM PANDA PARVATI! MOST PEOPLE JUST CALL ME PANDA. I WAS NAMED PANDA BECAUSE I RESEMBLE A PANDA BEAR WITH THE BLACK PATCHES AROUND MY EYES AND EARS, AND MY LEGS ARE BLACK. I AM CUTE AND HARMLESS LIKE A PANDA BEAR. HOWEVER, UNLIKE THE PANDA WHO EATS BAMBOO ALL DAY I PREFER FRESH GRASS FROM THE PASTURES OR DRIED GRASS IN THE FORM OF HAY. ALSO, I LOVE IT WHEN VISITORS BRING BREAD, SWEET RICE, VADU (A SAVORY DONUT), OR PAPAD (A THIN, CRISP, AND DISC-SHAPED FLATBREAD).

I LOVE MOO

HELLO MY NAME IS RADHARANI! I HAVE AN ITCH ON MY FACE SO I AM USING MY HIND HOOF TO SCRATCH IT. SOMETIMES I WILL USE A TREE STUMP, A FENCE, OR THE SIDE OF A BUILDING TO SCRATCH MY NECK, EARS OR FACE. IT HELPS GIVE ME SOME RELIEF AGAINST FLIES AND OTHER INSECTS. THE OTHER REMEDY IS HAVING SOMEONE BRUSH ME.

ONE DAY THIS SWEET VOLUNTEER GOPALA WAS BRUSHING ME. WHEN SHE WAS ABOUT TO BRUSH OTHER COWS I WOULD ASSERTIVELY SHOVE THEM OUT OF THE WAY. I WOULD MOVE TOWARD GOPALA AND GENTLY NUDGE HER IN THE SHOULDER WITH MY HEAD AND MOO. SHE LAUGHED AND GRINNED WIDELY AT ME, AND KEPT BRUSHING. SHE BRUSHED MY BACK, SHOULDERS, BEHIND MY EARS, AND MY HEAD AND LEGS.

IT FELT MOO-TASTIC! ANY TIME SHE WAS ABOUT TO STOP I WOULD SOFTLY NUDGE HER AGAIN. I WAS GOING TO MILK HER FOR ALL SHE'S WORTH BECAUSE SHE WAS GIVING ME THE ROYAL SPA TREATMENT!

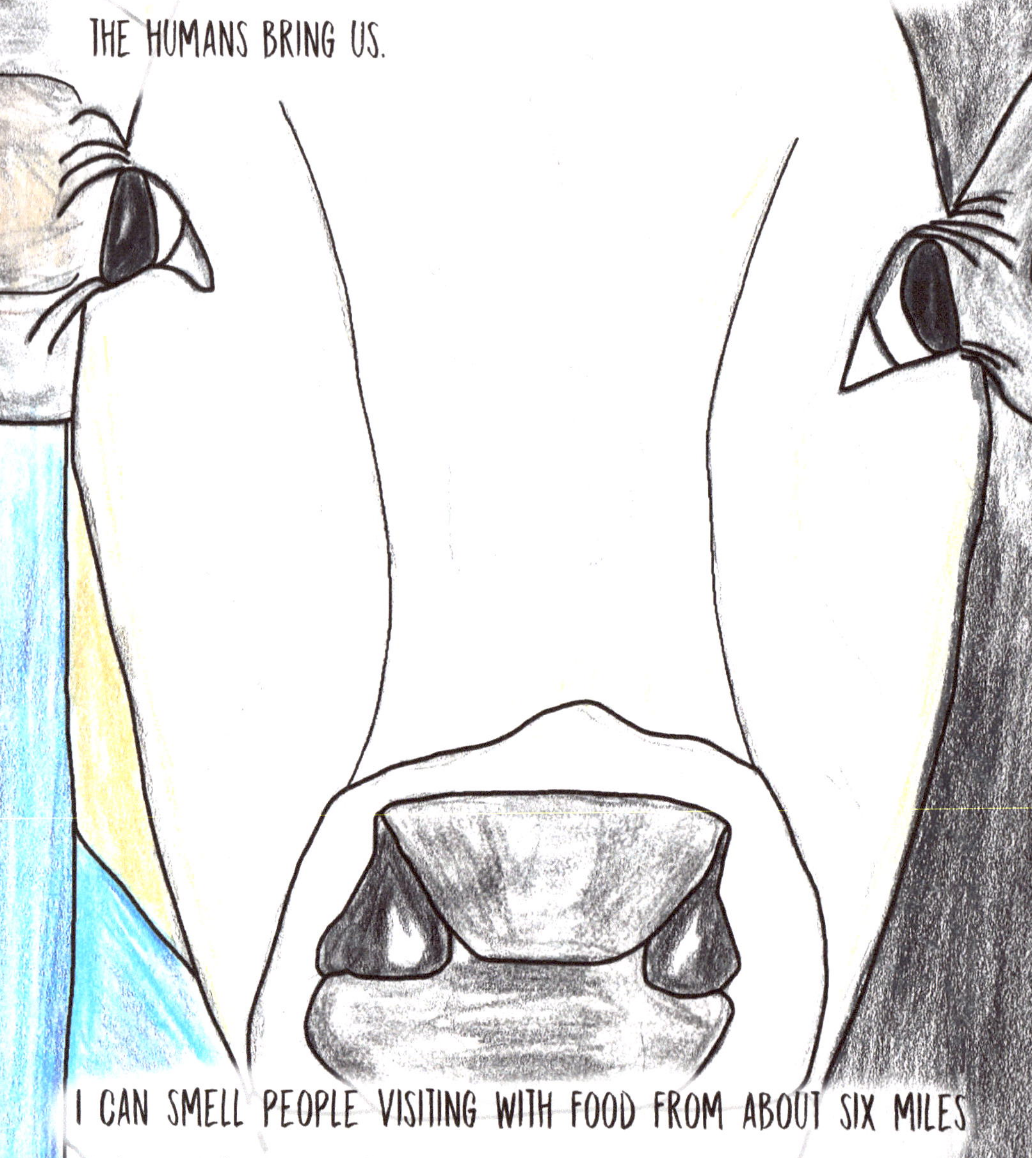

NAMASTE! MY NAME IS PARVATI. I AM MUNCHING ON SOME FRESH MORNING BREAKFAST HAY. IT IS MOO-TASTIC! THIS MORNING IS WARM AND SUNNY. SUNNY DAYS MAKE ME FEEL VERY HAPPY! THE SUNSHINE BRINGS OUT THE BEST IN ME, AND THE WONDERFUL TREATS THE HUMANS BRING US.

I CAN SMELL PEOPLE VISITING WITH FOOD FROM ABOUT SIX MILES AWAY. I AM ALWAYS READY TO RECEIVE THEM AT THE DRIVEWAY WHEN THEY ARRIVE.

SERIOUSLY KAMADHENU I AM NOT HEAD-BUTTING WITH YOU! RELAX! THERE IS NO NEED TO FEEL THREATENED. I AM STEPPING AWAY FROM YOUR BABY CALF TULSI RIGHT NOW.
I AM RAMA THE BRAHMA BULL. I MAY HAVE A HUMP ON MY BACK, BUT I DON'T HAVE A CHIP ON MY SHOULDER...SO LIGHTEN UP MAMA-KHAMA-DHENU!

WE ARE KRISHNA AND RAMA. WE OFTEN HEAR THE VOLUNTEER RAD-
HIKA CHANTING OUR NAME WITH DEVOTION. WE ALWAYS COME UP TO
HER AND QUIETLY LISTEN WHILE SHE IS HOLDING JAPA MEDITATION
BEADS IN HER HAND CHANTING THE FOLLOWING MANTRA:

HARE KRISHNA HARE KRISHNA
KRISHNA KRISHNA HARE HARE
HARE RAMA HARE RAMA
RAMA RAMA HARE HARE

HELLO. I AM BABY KALI. I AM FINISHING
UP MY DINNER BEFORE I GO PLAY, AND
THEN I AM GOING TO HIT THE HAY.

HI. I AM SHARADA. I AM ONE OF THE COWS THAT GETS MILKED AT THE SANCTUARY. WHEN I DON'T FEEL LIKE BEING MILKED I WILL KICK THE BUCKET YOU ARE USING. I ENJOY THE EXPERIENCE OF BEING MILKED BY VOLUNTEERS WHO TAKE THE TIME TO LEARN HOW TO MILK ME PROPERLY AND WITH CARE.

I LOVE MOO

HI MY NAME IS KAUSHIKI (COW-SHE-KEY). I WAS THINKING ABOUT MY MOM SOORYA WHO DIED A COUPLE OF MONTHS AGO. I AM STILL FEELING SAD AND GRIEVING HER LOSS. I CONTINUE TO FEEL THE PAIN OF SEPARATION FROM HER. SHE WOULD SAY TO ME EVERY NIGHT "I LOVE YOU TO THE MOO-OON AND BACK KAUSHIKI!" SHE WAS SUCH A LOVING MOTHER TO ME.

WHEN SHE DIED THE LIVE-IN VOLUNTEERS SANKAR, EMILY, RACHEL, AND JESSE CREMATED MY MOM. ALL THE OTHER COWS IN THE HERD CLUSTERED AROUND HER CREMATION SITE TO PAY THEIR RESPECTS AND MOURN HER LOSS. HER BODY WAS CONTINUOUSLY COVERED WITH WOOD AND GHEE, AND KEPT BURNING THROUGHOUT THE NIGHT TRANSFORMING TO ASH. I WAS BACK AND FORTH ALL DAY TO WATCH HER BODY DISAPPEAR AND PRAYED FOR HER SOUL TRANSITION. CRYSTAL DURGA WHO LOST HER MOM A FEW YEARS BACK STAYED BY MY SIDE ALL DAY TO COMFORT ME. SHE KNEW WHAT I WAS GOING THROUGH AND COULD EMPATHIZE WITH MY SITUATION. SHE IS MY BEST FRIEND AMONG THE HERD!

THE VOLUNTEERS WORKED VERY HARD THAT DAY. THEY HAULED WOOD BACK AND FORTH ON SLEDS TO COVER MY MOM'S BODY. THEY CIRCUMAMBULATED HER BODY AND CHANTED THE HARE KRISHNA MAHA-MANTRA. THE HIGHER VIBRATIONAL FREQUENCY OF THE HOLY NAMES OF GOD SURROUNDED MY MOM'S BODY WHILE HER SOUL TRANSITIONED TO THE HEAVENLY REALMS.

BLESSINGS! I AM VISHNU RED. MY NICKNAME IS BIG RED. I AM VERY STRONG AND WEIGH ABOUT 1500 POUNDS. I AM THE LEADER AMONG THE PECKING ORDER OF THE HERD. THE OTHER COWS LISTEN TO ME. THEY NEVER TRY TO SHOVE ME OUT OF THE WAY LIKE THEY DO EACH OTHER SOMETIMES DURING MEALS. THEY KNOW I AM THE MOST DOMI-NANT ONE IN THE HERD. I AM THE STRONGEST AND UNMOVABLE. SOMETIMES IT LOOKS LIKE THE HERD IS PLAYING MUSICAL CHAIRS.

IT IS COMPLETELY UNNECESSARY TO SHOVE EACH OTHER AND REAR-RANGE THE ORDER OF WHERE WE STAND TO EAT GRAIN AND HAY. THERE IS PLENTY TO MUNCH ON FOR ALL OF US! THEY CAN FOLLOW MY LEAD AND STAY CALM. I LIKE PEACE AND HARMONY, AND TO MAINTAIN ORDER AT THE SANCTUARY. I HOPE YOU CAN VISIT ME SOON! IT WOULD BE MOO-VELOUS!

I LOVE MOO

www.ingramcontent.com/pod-product-compliance
Lightning Source LLC
Chambersburg PA
CBHW040243240726
48664CB00001B/245